THE EMOTIONS BEHIND WEALTH

The impact of unhealthy attachment styles on business success

SHANE "THE NEGOTIATOR "HARRIS

Copyright © 2023 Shane Harris.

All rights reserved. No part of this publication may be reproduced, distributed, or transmitted in any form or by any means, including photocopying, recording, or other electronic or mechanical methods, without the prior written permission of the publisher, except in the case of brief quotations embodied in critical reviews and certain other noncommercial uses permitted by copyright law. For permission requests, please contact the author by visiting the following site: www.profitfirsttaxes.com

ISBN: 979-8-9885182-0-4 (Paperback)

Library of Congress – 2023910426

First printing edition 2023, USA

Giants and Geniuses Publishing LLC

Atlanta, GA

Dedication

My heartfelt dedication, acknowledging the resilience and perseverance despite the hardships you may have faced. I am dedicating this book to the inner child, both mine and yours. The journey that has been traveled to arrive at this point in life.

Acknowledgement

My acknowledgment is a testament to my gratitude and appreciation for the people who have played a part in shaping who I am today. It reflects my ability to recognize that everyone has contributed to my growth and development regardless of their impact. Acknowledging positive and negative influences shows you understand that challenges and difficulties can be valuable learning experiences. Your words also demonstrate a willingness to move forward with humility and respect for the people in your life.

Table of Contents

Dedication vii
Acknowledgement 8
CHAPTER ONE | HOW IT BEGAN 10
CHAPTER TWO | THE HOMEFRONT 15
CHAPTER THREE | THE SCHOOL YEARS 18
CHAPTER FOUR | EDUCATING SHANE 23
CHAPTER FIVE | The Attachment Style Theory 26
CHAPTER SIX | Fearful Avoidant Attachment Style 30
Checklist 32
CHAPTER SEVEN | Anxious Preoccupied Attachment Style 33
Checklist 36
CHAPTER EIGHT | Dismissive Avoidant Attachment Style 38
Checklist 40
CHAPTER NINE | How The Styles Effect US 41
Checklist and superpowers: 50
CHAPTER TEN | Overcoming Unhealthy Attachment Styles as an Entrepreneur 52
CHAPTER EVELEN | The Conclusion 67
Self-Reflection Checklist... 69
Journaling 74
References 87
About the Author 92
A Gift for YOU! 96

CHAPTER ONE | HOW IT BEGAN

The story begins with me, so let's begin. I was born in Guyana, which is in South America, not to be confused with Ghana, Africa – now that the geography lesson is out of the way, let us continue.

I was a happy, loving baby and toddler and had a close bond with my mother. When I was two years old, my mother and father migrated to the United States – New York, to be exact. I remained in Guyana with my maternal grandparents, aunts, and uncle.

You can imagine how devastating that was for me as a 2-year-old being separated from my mother. I was too young to remember the experience consciously, but I am positive I was affected somehow. I was the first and only daughter to my mother, grandchild to my grandparents, and niece to my aunts and uncle. My male cousin came along sometime around the age of two.

My mother called when she could and wrote letters; she didn't completely disappear. I knew my mother was my mother, but everyone called her by her first name, and so did I. I am sure it was cute too. I knew my grandmother was my grandmother, but since everyone else called her mommy, I naturally did.

I came home from school when I was four and discovered a little sister. Woah! Hold up, say what now? A 9-month-old baby greeted me, and I was baffled. My mother sent her to Guyana as it was easier for childcare purposes since she worked in the United States. When I went to school, it was only my male cousin and me; where did this little girl come from? She needed to leave! Those were my thoughts. I remember someone saying, "This is your little sister; you're not the baby anymore." Followed by "Don't be jealous." I can't recall if I understood what all this meant, but as time passed and she didn't leave, I figured we were keeping her.

The dynamic began shifting in my environment as I was used to being the first and only girl; now, I am sharing my time and attention with another little girl, with whom everyone's attention is. Again, I am sure you can imagine how my 4-year-old self-perceived that.

At the age of six, my mother finally returned to Guyana. I am trying to remember if it was for a few weeks or months, but she was temporarily there to get my documents together for me to join her in the U.S. As I mentioned earlier, I knew she was my mother and spoke to her a few times a year. However, she has been gone for four years and was a stranger to me. My sister and my mother have fallen into familiar territory with each other, but for me, I was standoffish and didn't warm up as quickly.

I called my mother by her first name, but since she was away for so long, she likely needed me to call her mommy, and of course, I didn't. I was a stubborn kid, and it was uncomfortable for me. Once again, the integration could have been better, as none of the adults had the tools to integrate correctly. When she would attempt to hug me, I wouldn't hug her back, I was very distant towards her, and she felt rejected. The more rejected she felt, the angrier she got and the more distant I became.

I became resentful when I saw how loving she was towards my sister. She had no idea how to bond with me, so she ignored me most of the time. She eventually left to return to New York, and I cried to break my little heart when she left. As much as I rejected her, I loved her and wanted to go with her.

Almost two years later, I got my wish. At age 7, a month shy of my eighth birthday, my sister and I joined my parents in New York. It was in the middle of a snowstorm. My little face was freezing. Everything looked bigger, brighter, and different from what I was used to. As I sat down to my first meal, a chicken thigh and leg, my eyes widened in terror. The portions before me loomed larger than any I had ever experienced back in Guyana. I was in a new world and culture and moved in with strangers.

CHAPTER TWO | THE HOMEFRONT

After my migration to New York, I began to settle into my new life in this foreign country. I started school and was very shy. My home life seemed quiet as I went from a house with over eight people living in it to 4 now. The honeymoon period lasted for a few weeks, and what seemed like out of nowhere, my parents started arguing and fighting with each other.

My father was physically abusive to my mother, which terrified my sister and me. My mother would say or do something he didn't like, they would argue, and he would beat her endlessly. My sister and I would huddle in a corner, terrified. I had never witnessed domestic violence of this magnitude before then.

We lived in a studio apartment, and there was no place to retreat when they got into it. My sister and I were there to see every harsh word, punch, all anger, bitterness, and resentment they displayed toward each other. Sometimes we were placed in the middle, mainly I was.

My mother would say to turn the T.V. off, and my father would say to turn it back on. The ordeal would go on for a few minutes as I would listen to them both, but I knew what my father was capable of, so I would eventually let him get the final word and do what he asked and ignore my mother.

"My mother appeared to resent me even more."

I would prefer she give me the cold shoulder than possibly get punched in the face by my father, and I chose wisely. My father was never physically abusive to my sister or me, but when he spoke, it sent fear down my spine, and the thought of what he could do to me would make me comply. He was also emotionally abusive and neglectful.

My mother, on the other hand, was emotionally and physically abusive. She did not spare the rod. My mother beat me for just about anything. If I didn't get the answers to my homework correct, I didn't do something right, and I misbehaved in any way, I would expect to get hit and usually did.

I feared both of my parents as they were so unpredictable. A good day can turn sour in the blink of an eye. I became the caretaker to my sister as my mother worked and my father ran the streets.

CHAPTER THREE | THE SCHOOL YEARS

On my first day of school, they placed me in kindergarten. I was almost eight and spent an entire day with the babies. A teacher of mine attempted to correct things and put me in first grade the next day.

When I was in Guyana, I was in the 3rd grade. Since I was quiet, the culture was different, and I had a heavy Guyanese accent, I didn't do so well on the placement exam. Therefore, they felt the first grade was appropriate. After all, this was the 80s, and not enough teachers cared back then to recognize that the culture I came from differed from the one I am in now. Also, I am terrified!

I failed the 2nd grade and repeated yet another year.

The other kids picked on me because I was different. I was hit, kicked, spit on, pissed on, stabbed at, etc., no one helped me. I would complain to my parents –

my mother was too passive and didn't like confrontation, she couldn't or wouldn't help me. My father was doing his thing and didn't help me much either, but he did teach me how to fight! I was grateful to him, and I started defending myself. I fought almost every day in school until the 5th grade when things slowed down.

I wasn't safe at home, and I wasn't safe at school. I was in a constant state of fear. There was no one I could speak to about the anger and rage building up inside me. No one protected me from all this violence; I had to defend myself.

This anger remained inside me throughout my childhood. We moved every year or so, which made it hard to make sustainable friendships. I was the new kid every time we moved. My parents parted ways when I was 10, and my grandmother came to the U.S. to live with us. My father didn't want to move, so he stayed, and we moved. It was the happiest day of my life—no more domestic violence. In the 5th grade, we stopped moving every year and finally, I started making friends.

But, this book isn't just about *my story*, so I will quickly summarize the remainder of my childhood.

Throughout middle and high school, I had many friends. I learned that people like humor, so I would make everyone laugh. People don't usually want to hit you if you're making them laugh. I loved to be active, so I played all kinds of sports. Track and Field was my favorite. My relationship with my father was estranged, as I barely saw him. He made promises he didn't keep and was not an active parent in my life. My mother and grandmother took care of me. They fed, clothed me, and provided a roof over my head. As for emotional support, I was on my own with that. I learned not to burden my family with my wants and needs and to keep them to myself. I valued my friendships more than anything because they met my emotional needs.

When I entered the 6th grade, my principal realized how smart I was and that I was two years older than everyone else and offered to skip two classes. I would have been placed in the 8th grade, meaning I would have spent one year in middle and then high school the following year. I quickly assessed the situation and declined. Here's my reason why; I had just started making friends the year prior, and skipping two grades would make me the new kid again. I'd probably be fighting every single day all over again. Nah, that was too many changes for me, and my trauma response was nope, let me stay here. No, thank you!

I graduated High School when I was 20 years old. I was two years older than my friends and classmates. I was legally 20, but my mentality was that of a 17 or 18-year-old. I joined the military and exited my mother's house three weeks after High school. *Now, what does this have to do with the price of tea in China?* You are about to find out in the next few chapters.

CHAPTER FOUR | EDUCATING SHANE

I see a good amount of social media posts with the statement stop operating in lack. What does that even mean? A person deemed to work with a lack mindset does so for fear of not having enough time, money, connections, rest, love, scarcity, and happiness. This list can go on forever, but you get the gist of it. According to Forbes, here are some tips to counter lack.

1. Focus on what you have.
2. Keep company with people who have an abundance mindset.
3. Create win-win situations.
4. Incorporate gratitude into your daily life.
5. Train your mind to recognize possibilities.

The previous list is excellent; for many people, you can overcome a lack mentality and start living more abundantly. For others, nothing seems to improve that mindset, no matter how much you attempt to change your thinking. Likely, you will still need help seeing the business growth you desire. Positive affirmations, manifestations, prayer, and any other similar tool you may use will likely not work as it specifically targets the conscious mind but does nothing for the subconscious or unconscious mind. The subconscious mind is the problem and that is the area that you would need to tap into and heal for the affirmations to actually work. It would help if you reprogrammed the subconscious.

You may or may not have heard of something called attachment styles. If you do some research or Google, these styles center around romantic relationships.

However, they play out in all relationship types; Romantic, family, friends, and for the sake of this book, relationships with money and your business. As we go through the different types, we will reference the list and my story from the beginning of the book to see the correlations.

There is a quote that says, *"How you do anything is how you do everything"*, it's about having a powerhouse mindset.

"If your attitude about the product or service you are delivering is, "That's good enough" or "No one will notice my mistake." You are telling others, perhaps subconsciously, that you don't really respect your own work", according to Martha Beck.

In other words, if you are operating your personal life, relationships, and finances in an unhealthy way, you will also manage your business relationships and finances in a harmful way.

CHAPTER FIVE | The Attachment Style Theory

Attachment theory is a psychological explanation for people's emotional bonds and relationships. It focuses on the relationships and bonds between individuals, particularly long-term relationships such as those between a parent and child and between romantic partners [1].

According to attachment theory, these relationships are essential for human survival and development, providing individuals with security, comfort, and support [2]. The theory was first proposed by John Bowlby, a British psychoanalyst, in the 1950s and has since become an important concept in psychology [3].

Attachment theory is essential in psychology because it helps us understand how early childhood experiences can shape how individuals form and maintain relationships throughout their lives [4]. Research on adult attachment guides by the assumption that the same motivational system that gives rise to the close emotional bond between parents and their children also influences the formation and maintenance of intimate relationships in adulthood [5]. Thus, attachment theory provides a framework for understanding the importance of relationships in human development and well-being [6].

There are four main attachment styles: secure, anxious-preoccupied, dismissive-avoidant, and fearful-avoidant [2]. Each class is associated with different patterns of behavior and emotions in relationships and can positively and negatively affect individuals' well-being and the quality of their relationships [6]. These attachment styles can profoundly affect an individual's personal and professional life, including their success as an entrepreneur.

Research has shown that an individual's attachment style can impact their agency and business development, whether they know it or not [2]. You are likely intrigued.

Understanding attachment styles is crucial in business, as it can impact an entrepreneur's ability to form and maintain successful partnerships and collaborations. According to attachment theory, individuals with a secure attachment style are more likely to develop healthy relationships, while those with an insecure attachment style may struggle with trust and intimacy [3]. This unhealthy style can lead to difficulties forming and maintaining business relationships, ultimately impacting an entrepreneur's success.

Unhealthy attachment styles can hurt an entrepreneur's mental health and overall well-being, affecting their ability to succeed in their business ventures.

Research has shown that having an insecure attachment style can lead to negative relationship experiences and impact overall well-being [4]. Additionally, studies have examined the effect of attachment patterns on entrepreneurial tendency, suggesting that attachment styles may affect an individual's likelihood of becoming an entrepreneur [3].

Therefore, understanding and addressing attachment styles can significantly impact an entrepreneur's personal and professional success.

CHAPTER SIX | Fearful Avoidant Attachment Style

Individuals with a fearful avoidant attachment style tend to have conflicting desires for intimacy and independence, resulting in difficulty forming and maintaining close relationships [2]. Characteristics of this attachment style include a fear of rejection, mistrust of others, and a tendency to withdraw when feeling overwhelmed [1]. These individuals often struggle to express emotions and may avoid close relationships altogether [5].

For entrepreneurs, a fearful avoidant attachment style can significantly impact their ability to form and maintain business relationships. This attachment style can lead to difficulty trusting others, making it challenging to create partnerships or delegate tasks to others [3]. Additionally, the tendency to withdraw when feeling overwhelmed can lead to avoidance of necessary tasks or decision-making, ultimately hindering business growth and success [2].

There are several examples of how a fearful avoidant attachment style can manifest in entrepreneurs. For instance, an entrepreneur with this attachment style may struggle to form close relationships with clients or employees, leading to difficulty retaining business [2]. Additionally, they may avoid seeking help or support from others, leading to burnout or a lack of innovation in their business [3]. Understanding one's attachment style and how it impacts entrepreneurial tendencies can lead to improved self-awareness and business success [6].

Checklist
- ☐ hesitant to share deep feelings
- ☐ stay in relationships longer than necessary
- ☐ anxiety
- ☐ low self-esteem
- ☐ poor view of others
- ☐ desire to get emotional needs met in a relationship
- ☐ desire not to get hurt
- ☐ hesitant in starting new things
- ☐ struggle to maintain business relationships
- ☐ desire intimacy and fight for independence
- ☐ fear of rejection
- ☐ fear of abandonment
- ☐ difficulty trusting others
- ☐ poor decision-making when overwhelmed
- ☐ avoid tasks when stressed
- ☐ avoid asking for help or support
- ☐ emotionally withdraw when overwhelmed

Does any of this sound familiar to you?

CHAPTER SEVEN | Anxious Preoccupied Attachment Style

Anxious Preoccupied Attachment Style is a form of insecure attachment that often manifests from inconsistent parenting [7]. Individuals with this attachment style tend to be more nervous about relationships, crave intimacy, and are more likely to be needy or jealous [2]. Characteristics of an Anxious, Preoccupied Attachment Style include an intense fear of abandonment, preoccupation with relationships, and a tendency to overthink and overanalyze [1]. These individuals often seek constant reassurance from their partners and may become overly dependent on them.

Anxious Preoccupied Attachment Style can have a significant impact on entrepreneurs. Studies suggest that attachment patterns can influence entrepreneurial tendencies [3] and that attachment style can moderate the association between excessive reassurance-seeking behavior and entrepreneurial success [8]. Entrepreneurs with an Anxious, Preoccupied Attachment Style may struggle with decision-making and risk-taking, as they may be more prone to overthinking and doubt. They may also need help with delegation and collaboration, as they may have difficulty trusting others and feel the need to control every aspect of their business [2].

Examples of Anxious, Preoccupied Attachment Styles in Entrepreneurs include being overly sensitive to criticism or rejection, being excessively self-critical, and having difficulty separating personal and professional relationships [2]. Female entrepreneurs with high entrepreneurial orientation tend to have an anxious attachment style, while male entrepreneurs with high entrepreneurial orientation tend to have a secure attachment style [9]. Entrepreneurs with an Anxious, Preoccupied Attachment Style may benefit from seeking therapy or coaching to address their attachment patterns and learn healthier ways of building relationships and running their businesses [10][8][3].

Checklist
- [ ] difficulty trusting others
- [ ] low self-worth
- [ ] worries that your partners will abandon you
- [ ] craving closeness and intimacy
- [ ] being overly dependent in relationships
- [ ] requiring frequent reassurance that people care about you
- [ ] being overly sensitive to a partner's actions and moods
- [ ] being highly emotional, impulsive, unpredictable, and moody
- [ ] clingy or needy
- [ ] analyze and overthink the meaning behind what others do and speak
- [ ] anxious and stressed, often
- [ ] people pleasing
- [ ] poor boundaries or no boundaries
- [ ] giving too much time and attention to others
- [ ] putting the self-first is not a priority
- [ ] controlling

- ☐ excessive attention seeking
- ☐ jealousy
- ☐ under appreciated
- ☐ dissatisfied
- ☐ fear of abandonment
- ☐ fear of rejection
- ☐ hypersensitivity to criticism

Does any of this sound familiar to you?

CHAPTER EIGHT | Dismissive Avoidant Attachment Style

The dismissive avoidant attachment style signalizes a tendency to avoid close relationships and emotions. Individuals with this attachment style often have a high degree of self-reliance and independence but also tend to avoid emotional intimacy and vulnerability [11]. This attachment style is developed in childhood and can manifest in adulthood as a fear or uncertainty in relationships [12].

The dismissive avoidant attachment style can have a significant impact on entrepreneurs. While their self-reliance and independence can benefit the workplace, their avoidance of emotional intimacy and vulnerability can hinder their ability to form strong relationships with business partners, investors, and customers, leading to missed opportunities and difficulties in building a successful business [2].

Examples of dismissive avoidant attachment styles in entrepreneurs include a reluctance to seek help or advice from others, avoiding emotional discussions or conflicts with business partners, and preferring to work alone rather than in a team [13]. Entrepreneurs must recognize their attachment style and how it may impact their business relationships to develop strategies for building stronger connections and achieving success in their ventures.

Checklist

- ☐ dismissive attitude
- ☐ negative emotions
- ☐ prefer to work alone, dislikes group
- ☐ distant; use work commitment to avoid socializing
- ☐ opposing views and criticism towards the leaders and authority
- ☐ resistant to authority and new information
- ☐ distrust towards others in general and towards the authority
- ☐ don't ask for help or advice
- ☐ avoid emotional discussions
- ☐ confident (external only)
- ☐ don't trust other
- ☐ fear of rejection
- ☐ fear of abandonment

Does any of this sound familiar to you?

CHAPTER NINE | How The Styles Effect US

How these unhealthy styles correlate with my story (of yours)?

Based on the attachment style theory, unhealthy attachment styles comes from childhood trauma, although they can also come from adult traumas. I was separated from my parents very early, without knowing when and if reunification would occur. Fear of abandonment and trust issues became the result. The children in my schools picked on and bullied me for several years, in addition to my parents fighting and arguing constantly.

I did not feel safe in school or at home.

I felt like I had no one to turn to for help. Feeling unsafe caused me to have a mix of all the unhealthy attachment styles we previously discussed. I became as small as possible in my household, not wanting to draw any attention to myself. I followed the rules, earned my keep, and became very good at reading people and their emotions. When I walked into my home, I knew if it would be a good or bad day, and I would adjust to whichever.

      I initially kept to myself at school and with friends, which displayed more avoidance. However, I soon discovered you could catch more bees with honey; therefore, I became funny and entertaining, which equates to pleasing people. I knew what people wanted and needed and could give them without asking. I was hypersensitive to my environment and always scanned for threats. Although I had poor boundaries, I never gave in to peer pressure. I knew right from wrong and avoided displeasing adults and people of authority. Depending on the situation, I flip-flopped between attachment styles, a subconscious response.

Since I had no one to protect me, I had to defend myself, so adapting to my environment allowed me to survive my childhood, and of course, it poured into adulthood. Since I am like a chameleon and can flip-flop between these styles, I have always been successful in my career and business. It isn't always a bed of roses because although I can excel and be a high achiever in work and business, I struggled for over 30 years with maintaining healthy friendships and relationships. I also wouldn't stayed at one job for more than two years, as I would move on to another. I also had multiple jobs, not because I needed the money, but because I had another on standby just in case I decided to do a "F" it I'm out. My work relationships remained at work, and my private life stayed at home, and the few people I trusted enough to let in.

I was 38 years old when my life hit rock bottom and I decided what I was doing wasn't working, and I had to do something different. I then began doing the opposite of every unhealthy habit I had. As a result, it has led me down the path to a more secure attachment style.

I will not say I am 100% secure because I am not. I am continuously working on improving myself and helping others through my experiences. For every negative, there is usually some positive. Unhealthy attachment styles are okay. As you have learned, I had to adapt to my environment to survive and function, and I have listed a few of my superpowers. You also have superpowers based on your unhealthy attachment styles.

Wait! There is hope for all of us – the superpowers are available.

Anxious attachment styles superpower
- natural lie detectors (Can pick up quickly on deception)
- self-aware
- problem solver
- easy to work with
- people trust you
- alert to surroundings
- fastest in detecting threat
- empathetic
- always looking for ways to improve self and tasks
- can function under high pressure for extended periods

Avoidant attachment style superpowers
- intense focus on tasks
- drive for success
- in times of danger, respond the quickest and most efficiently without much hesitation
- work well independently
- finish tasks

Fearful avoidants combine anxious and avoidant superpowers, making it harder for others to read and predict. Your poker face can help you succeed in business.

Secure Attachment Style

This attachment style is marked by a positive view of oneself, others, and relationships. Securely attached individuals tend to have trust, lasting relationships, good self-esteem, and no difficulty sharing feelings with their partners and friends. This attachment style typically develops in children whose caregivers are warm, responsive, and consistently meet their needs [10].

Attachment theory is essential in psychology because it helps explain how early experiences can shape an individual's personality and behavior in adulthood. People with a secure attachment style are typically warm, loving, and capable of building and maintaining healthy relationships [11]. They are comfortable being alone and independent but enjoy close connections with others [12]. In contrast, individuals with insecure attachment styles may struggle with trust, intimacy, and emotional regulation in their relationships [13].

A secure attachment style is crucial in promoting healthy relationships and overall well-being. Securely attached individuals experience less anxiety and avoidance in their relationships [9]. They are comfortable giving and receiving love and can trust others [13]. This attachment style is also associated with greater relationship satisfaction and a lower risk of mental health issues such as anxiety and depression [14]. Therefore, understanding attachment theory and developing a secure attachment style can lead to healthier and more fulfilling relationships.

Entrepreneurs with a secure attachment style have several key characteristics that benefit their businesses. They are more likely to be resilient in the face of setbacks, able to take calculated risks, and have a strong sense of self-efficacy [12]. They can also better adapt to changing circumstances and make decisions based on rational thinking rather than emotional reactions [9]. These characteristics are essential for success in the entrepreneurial world, where uncertainty and risk-taking are commonplace.

Examples of entrepreneurs with a secure attachment style include Richard Branson, founder of the Virgin Group, and Sara Blakely, founder of Spanx. Branson and Blakely have demonstrated the ability to take risks, adapt to changing circumstances, and form strong relationships with employees and business partners [3]. In contrast, entrepreneurs with insecure attachment styles may struggle to create and maintain relationships, have difficulty trusting others, and may be more prone to anxiety and depression [14]. Thus, developing a secure attachment style can be a valuable asset for entrepreneurs looking to succeed in the business world.

Checklist and superpowers:
- [ ] optimistic view of self & others
- [ ] healthy self-esteem
- [ ] comfortable with intimacy and close relationships
- [ ] self-sufficient & comfortable seeking support
- [ ] ease with emotional closeness
- [ ] warm to others
- [ ] can and will trust others
- [ ] ability to regulate emotions
- [ ] confidence is self, welcomes constructive criticism and feedback
- [ ] assertive
- [ ] set healthy boundaries
- [ ] comfortable and capable of forming solid bonds
- [ ] comfortable in group settings
- [ ] less likely to fear rejection
- [ ] higher satisfaction with work
- [ ] trust leadership and authority
- [ ] less likely to have symptoms of physical and mental health illnesses

- ☐ good self-esteem
- ☐ comfortable sharing feelings with partners and friends

CHAPTER TEN | Overcoming Unhealthy Attachment Styles as an Entrepreneur

Becoming a secure entrepreneur requires effective risk management and mitigation strategies. They identify potential risks and develop plans to prevent or minimize their impact on the business. One way to achieve this is through enterprise risk management, which consists of identifying and assessing risks, implementing risk mitigation strategies, and monitoring and reporting risk levels [15]. Other effective risk management strategies include choosing the correct entity, obtaining appropriate insurance policies, creating disaster preparedness plans, and establishing contracts and agreements [16]. Entrepreneurs should pay themselves, keep good credit, monitor their books, and plan to manage their company's finances [25]. Effective financial management is vital for business survival and growth [26].

Additionally, money management is crucial for entrepreneurs to manage their finances and their company's resources and assets [27]. By implementing sound financial management practices, entrepreneurs can ensure the long-term financial stability of their businesses. By implementing these strategies, entrepreneurs can minimize the potential impact of risks and ensure the long-term success of their business [17].

Building a solid support system is also essential for becoming a secure entrepreneur. Surrounding oneself with other business owners, mentors, and professionals in other industries [18]. A strong support network can provide guidance, advice, and resources to help entrepreneurs navigate the challenges of starting and growing a business [19].

Additionally, having a support system can help entrepreneurs maintain their confidence and motivation, which is crucial for achieving success [20]. Entrepreneurial support systems generate community benefits by promoting collaboration and economic development [21]. By building a solid support system, entrepreneurs can increase their chances of success and ensure the long-term stability of their businesses.

Another key strategy for becoming a secure entrepreneur is continual learning and adaptation. In today's fast-paced business environment, it is essential to continually learn and adapt to new challenges and opportunities [22]. Embrace continuous change, analyzing, innovating, designing, and evolving strategies [23]. By adopting a culture of constant learning, entrepreneurs can stay ahead of the competition, identify new trends and opportunities, and ensure the long-term success of their business [24]. Adaptive companies are learning how to push activities outside the company, without benefiting competitors and how to design and evolve strategies [25]. Therefore, entrepreneurs should prioritize continual learning and adaptation to ensure their businesses' long-term success and security [26].

The Impact of Unhealthy Attachment Styles on Entrepreneurial Success

Unhealthy attachment styles can have a significant impact on entrepreneurial success. Research has shown that attachment patterns can affect entrepreneurial tendencies, with individuals who have unhealthy attachment styles being less likely to succeed in their entrepreneurial endeavors [3]. Unhealthy attachment styles can hinder entrepreneurial success by impacting an individual's ability to make critical decisions, take risks, and form meaningful relationships with business partners and customers [2].

For example, individuals with an anxious-preoccupied attachment style may overreact to setbacks or become overwhelmed by stressors, which can impede their ability to make effective decisions in their business [10]. As a result, addressing and overcoming unhealthy attachment styles is crucial for entrepreneurial success [15].

There are several examples of successful entrepreneurs who struggle with unhealthy attachment styles. For instance, individuals with an avoidant attachment style tend to prefer working independently in order to avoid developing deep emotional connections with partners. This inclination can pose challenges for them when it comes to establishing strong relationships with both customers and employees. [12]. Additionally, individuals with a disorganized attachment style may need help with impulsivity and emotional regulation, which can hinder their ability to make sound business decisions [16].

Despite these challenges, individuals with unhealthy attachment styles can succeed in entrepreneurship by addressing and overcoming their attachment patterns [2].
Addressing unhealthy attachment styles is essential for entrepreneurial success. By recognizing and addressing attachment patterns, individuals can develop the emotional intelligence and self-awareness necessary to form healthy relationships with business partners and customers [17].

Addressing unhealthy attachment styles can also help individuals build resilience and make effective decisions under stress [18]. While addressing unhealthy attachment styles may require significant effort and self-reflection, it is crucial to achieving entrepreneurial success [14].

Anxious Preoccupied to Secure Attachment Activities

These activities for entrepreneurs have become increasingly popular in recent years. They offer an opportunity to learn strategies to help promote healthier relationships with colleagues, employees, and clients. For entrepreneurs, anxiety and preoccupation with relationships can significantly impede success. Anxious Preoccupied to Secure Attachment Activities provide an opportunity to manage the emotions and worries associated with relationships. By participating in these activities, entrepreneurs can learn to identify their needs, recognize their feelings, and understand the feelings of others. With this understanding, entrepreneurs can develop healthier and more productive relationships with their business partners, clients, and employees. An essential part of Anxious Preoccupied to Secure Attachment Activities is learning how to process emotions constructively.

Through these activities, entrepreneurs can learn to recognize when they are anxious or preoccupied and use techniques to reduce those feelings and improve their ability to connect with others. Such strategies could include breathing exercises, visualization, mindfulness, and journaling.

For entrepreneurs looking to take advantage of these activities, various options are available. For example, one popular activity is emotional regulation. It focuses on helping entrepreneurs identify and manage their emotions to navigate relationships and potential conflicts better. Additionally, secure attachment activities can help build trust, openness, and connection with others. One way to practice emotional regulation is to journal your feelings and thoughts through a stream of consciousness or by focusing on a particular emotion or situation. Writing down your thoughts can help you to process and manage your feelings.

Additionally, practicing mindfulness techniques, like meditation or yoga, can help entrepreneurs focus on the present moment and manage their emotions.

Developing secure attachment activities can be a helpful strategy for entrepreneurs to manage their anxious and preoccupied thoughts better. Creating a plan of action that includes self-care activities is a great way to start—designating time to enjoy a hobby, taking regular breaks during the day, and getting enough sleep. Additionally, engaging in activities that promote physical, mental, and emotional well-being can help entrepreneurs stay healthy and balanced. One helpful way to promote secure attachment is to practice mindful communication.

Listen attentively to conversations, speak calmly, and respond with empathy. Practicing this type of communication can help entrepreneurs to be aware of their own and others' feelings and build stronger connections with colleagues and customers. Additionally, taking the time to cultivate meaningful relationships with employees, partners, and clients can be an effective way for entrepreneurs to establish secure attachments. Engaging in activities that promote security and trustworthiness can help entrepreneurs to build substantial extensions with others—being more mindful of their words when communicating, being honest and trustworthy, and taking the time to listen to others and validate their thoughts and feelings.

Furthermore, entrepreneurs should be aware of the power of their presence and use it to their advantage. Entrepreneurs can develop a strong sense of attachment and security by being authentic and open to others, expressing themselves honestly, being vulnerable, and allowing others to see their true selves. Additionally, entrepreneurs should be conscious of how their body language affects their relationships and try to connect with those around them. One way to start developing secure attachment activities is to create a daily schedule that includes time for self-care.

Exercise, meditation, or reading. Setting aside time to connect with friends and family is also essential. Schedule regular calls, send text messages, or set up virtual hangouts. Additionally, entrepreneurs should attend events or activities related to their interests or passions.

Creating a sense of security and trust with those you are close to is vital for entrepreneurs, so it is crucial to participate in activities that can help them achieve this. For example, engaging in activities like volunteering or joining a support or interest group can help build meaningful relationships with those who can provide emotional and practical support.

Entrepreneurs should also explore preoccupied attachment activities such as journaling, yoga, and meditation. By engaging in these activities, entrepreneurs can learn to identify and manage their emotions, an invaluable skill, particularly in the early stages of a business. Journaling can help entrepreneurs to process their thoughts and feelings, while yoga and meditation can help them to achieve a sense of calm and relaxation.

Taking time out and connecting with nature can also help entrepreneurs to balance their emotions and thoughts. Going for a walk in the park or to the beach can provide some much-needed respite and clarity. Talking with a close friend or family can offer security and relief from anxious, preoccupied thoughts. It is important to remember that it is business and not personal. If a client is critical of your business, products, or services, it is best not to take it as a personal attack.

These activities can also help entrepreneurs to develop secure attachment patterns. Secure attachment patterns refer to the ability to form meaningful and healthy relationships with others, even in the face of difficulty. By engaging in activities like mindfulness, self-reflection, and regular social interactions, entrepreneurs can learn to identify and manage their anxieties and preoccupations, allowing them to better connect with their colleagues, partners, and customers. Even if the relationships are positive and robust, setting healthy boundaries and remaining mindful of the business context can help entrepreneurs to stay focused and motivated. Engaging in certain attachment activities can also help entrepreneurs to understand their motivations and emotions in a more organized way, allowing them to find better and more efficient ways to reach their goals.

Some activities I engage in are journaling, listening to music, meditation, deep breathing exercises, and spending time in nature, as I enjoy hiking. I also process my thoughts with trusted and credible people that would give me honest feedback and not tell me what they think I want to hear. I sit with my thoughts and emotions for a few minutes up to a few days processing how and if I could have done things better. I am slower to react and less explosive than I once was as a child and in early adulthood. I also have an emotional support animal that helps me stay grounded, remain calm in stressful situations, and gives me unconditional love when needed. I have learned to regulate my emotions, provide self-love, and trust my intuition and instincts. Meet my needs, set better boundaries, become more assertive, stand confident in anything I do, and give myself grace when I have set back. One of the most important things I do is limit myself around negativity, including people and situations that will bring my mood down: family members, friends, relationships, clients, and colleagues. I sometimes need to isolate myself to recharge as I am an empath and absorb the energies of others around me.

I set alarms to remind me to take breaks throughout the day because as business owners we can get tunnel vision and forget about holidays. My phone goes on do not disturb at bedtime to eliminate distractions and promote a better night's rest. I set time aside for activities I enjoy and for fun times with friends. I only keep positive people in my circle, as negativity can spread like wildfire, which is detrimental while transitioning to a more secure attachment style. I also read self-help books and watch YouTube videos as therapy. I had a therapist for five years, the longest healthy relationship.

A few short weeks ago, I had my last session, as I felt she had gotten me as far as she could.

CHAPTER EVELEN | The Conclusion

Unhealthy attachment styles can impact entrepreneurs and their businesses. Research has shown that attachment styles can affect an entrepreneur's agency, business development, emotional rewards, and business relationships [2][17]. Insecure attachment styles, such as fearful-avoidant or anxious-preoccupied, can lead to difficulties in forming deep emotional and intimate connections with partners and colleagues [12][11]. Additionally, attachment styles can heavily influence self-worth and interpersonal trust, essential for success in entrepreneurship [23]. Thus, entrepreneurs must address and overcome unhealthy attachment styles that may hinder their personal and professional growth.

Encouragement to address and overcome unhealthy attachment styles is essential for entrepreneurs. These styles play a crucial role in entrepreneurship and can significantly impact an entrepreneur's personal and professional life.

Understanding and addressing unhealthy attachment styles can lead to increased self-awareness, emotional regulation, and better relationships. While it may be challenging to confront these patterns, seeking support from a therapist or coach can be beneficial in this process. By prioritizing their mental and emotional well-being, entrepreneurs can set themselves up for success in both their personal and professional lives.

Self-Reflection Checklist

I have created a checklist for self-reflection. How are you showing up in your business, and if you have checked off 1 or more items from the list, what are you going to do to improve yourself? Change starts when you recognize there is a problem and make the decision to do something about it. Almost every business owner want to make millions; those millions can be yours once you become a better you. Remember that Rome wasn't built in a day, so give yourself grace when you have a setback.

Make a mental note or check off all that apply.

- ☐ Started a business and within the first 1-3 years made over six figures only to hit a block, and the momentum to continue to scale began to decline despite your best efforts?
- ☐ Starting that business and soon after launch, you lose motivation to continue.
- ☐ Have so many great ideas to become an entrepreneur, but wait to act on them.
- ☐ Have inconsistencies in the amount of income your business makes.
- ☐ Struggle with your finances.
- ☐ Unable to maintain a budget.
- ☐ Overspending even if it is causing more financial hardship.
- ☐ Afraid or reluctant to delegate tasks in your business to reduce or eliminate your workload?
- ☐ Consistently give customers and clients huge discounts, which cut into your profits.

- Overextending yourself in and out of your business
- Constantly worrying about money.
- Don't worry enough about money and spend it like there is no tomorrow.
- Avoid filing your taxes for fear of owning.
- Do everything in your business and won't hire employees or contractors.
- Sit with financial advisors, Tax professionals, Accountants, CPAs, and E.A.s. Despite them showing you ways to save on taxes, better cash management, and ways they can help you grow your business, you don't commit to any ongoing services.
- Need to be more organized when it comes to finances.
- Fear of not having enough money
- Putting other people's needs before your own
- Not knowing what your needs are
- Live in fear of the past and the future.

- Spending more money than your business makes
- Stay in financial relationships with your accountant or tax professional due to loyalty, even when you know the relationship is hurting your business and finances.
- Anxious when it comes to dealing with taxes and finances.
- Avoid legal and financial matters in your business.
- Have trouble setting boundaries with clients.
- Difficulty connecting with clients.
- Poor self-esteem
- Confident outwardly with poor confidence inward
- Refrain from following up with clients.
- Avoid conflict
- Afraid to let go of demanding clients
- Stay in situations longer than you should
- Ignore important documents.
- Poor personal and business finances

- ☐ Have difficulty networking.
- ☐ Always worrying about money
- ☐ Afraid or hesitant to charge your worth
- ☐ Poor decision-making skills
- ☐ Need approval from others when producing business ideas.
- ☐ Afraid to open mail from creditors and the IRS

I am certain that after reading this book you have tapped into something that will help you not only become a better business owner/entrepreneur but a better you.

Take a few moments to see your Attachment style assessment if you haven't already figured it out.

https://attachment.personaldevelopmentschool.com/

Journaling

Reflect on the book and explore your own perspective on the relationship between emotional well-being, attachment styles, and financial success in the business world. Consider the following questions as you delve into your thoughts and experiences.

Remember to approach these journal prompts with openness and honesty, allowing yourself to explore your thoughts, experiences, and emotions surrounding the relationship between attachment styles, emotions, and business success.

1. What are your initial thoughts and feelings when you encounter the phrase "emotions behind wealth"? How do you perceive the connection between emotions and financial success?

_____

_____

_____

_____

_____

_____

_____

_____

_____

_____

_____

_____

2. How does your attachment style influence your relationship with wealth and success? Reflect on your own attachment patterns and consider how they might impact your business endeavors.

_____

_____

_____

_____

_____

_____

_____

_____

_____

_____

_____

3. Are you driven by a fear of scarcity or a need for validation when pursuing wealth? Explore the emotions and motivations behind your pursuit of success and consider how they align with healthy attachment styles.

_____

_____

_____

_____

_____

_____

_____

_____

_____

_____

_____

_____

_____

4. How does an unhealthy attachment style impact your decision-making process in business? Reflect on instances where your attachment patterns may have influenced your choices, and consider alternative approaches that align with a healthier mindset.

_____
_____
_____
_____
_____
_____
_____
_____
_____
_____
_____
_____
_____

5. What emotions arise when you encounter setbacks or failures in your business endeavors? Reflect on how your attachment style affects your response to challenges and consider ways to cultivate resilience and adaptability.

_____

_____

_____

_____

_____

_____

_____

_____

_____

_____

_____

_____

6. How can you foster a healthier relationship with wealth and success? Reflect on strategies and practices that can help you develop a more secure attachment style and create a balanced approach to business and personal fulfillment.

_____
_____
_____
_____
_____
_____
_____
_____
_____
_____
_____
_____

References

1. How Attachment Styles Influence Managers & Entrepreneurs. https://medium.com/@theshaunagraham/how-attachment-styles-influence-managers-entrepreneurs-feac5f129a0b?source=rss-f54106acb15e------2 Accessed 2023-04-02
2. Could Your Attachment Style Impact Business Development?. https://klcampbell.com/could-your-attachment-style-impact-business-development/ Accessed 2023-04-02
3. Attachment Orientations and Entrepreneurial Tendencies. https://www.mdpi.com/2076-328X/13/1/61/pdf Accessed 2023-04-02
4. Attachment: The What, the Why, and the Long-Term Effects. https://kids.frontiersin.org/articles/10.3389/frym.2023.809060 Accessed 2023-04-02
5. The Superpowers of Fearful Avoidant Attachment. https://www.attachmentproject.com/blog/fearful-avoidant-disorganized-superpowers/ Accessed 2023-04-02

6. A Secure Base for Entrepreneurship: Attachment Orientations ....https://www.ncbi.nlm.nih.gov/pmc/articles/PMC9854824/ Accessed 2023-04-02
7. The Superpowers of Anxious Preoccupied Attachment.https://www.attachmentproject.com/blog/anxious-preoccupied-attachment-superpowers/ Accessed 2023-04-02
8. The Contribution of Attachment Styles and Reassurance ....https://www.ncbi.nlm.nih.gov/pmc/articles/PMC8895702/ Accessed 2023-04-02
9. Attachment, Anxiety and the Entrepreneurial Mind.https://research-repository.griffith.edu.au/handle/10072/367443?show=full Accessed 2023-04-02
10. How Attachment Styles Influence Managers & Entrepreneurs.https://medium.com/@theshaunagraham/how-attachment-styles-influence-managers-entrepreneurs-feac5f129a0b?source=rss------business-5 Accessed 2023-04-02
11. How Attachment Styles Affect Adult Relationships.https://www.helpguide.org/articles/relationships-communication/attachment-and-adult-relationships.htm Accessed 2023-04-02

12. Insecure Attachment Style: Behaviors, Causes & How To ....https://www.mindbodygreen.com/articles/insecure-attachment-style Accessed 2023-04-02

13. The Superpowers of Dismissive Avoidant Attachment.https://www.attachmentproject.com/blog/dismissive-avoidant-attachment-superpowers/ Accessed 2023-04-02

14. Impact of attachment, temperament and parenting on ....https://www.ncbi.nlm.nih.gov/pmc/articles/PMC3534157/ Accessed 2023-04-02

15. Attachment orientations and entrepreneurship | Request PDF.https://www.researchgate.net/publication/324215560_Attachment_orientations_and_entrepreneurship Accessed 2023-04-02

16. Attachment Theory: Bowlby and Ainsworth's ....https://www.verywellmind.com/what-is-attachment-theory-2795337 Accessed 2023-04-02

17. Why and how do founding entrepreneurs bond with their ....https://www.sciencedirect.com/science/article/pii/S0883902617302987 Accessed 2023-04-02

18. How your attachment style affects your relationship

....https://bossbabe.com/how-your-attachment-style-affects-your-relationship-with-men-and-money/ Accessed 2023-04-02

19. The Trust Issue That's Keeping You Stuck in Your Career ....https://www.muriellemarie.com/blog/the-trust-issue-thats-keeping-you-stuck-in-your-career-or-business-attachment-theory-and-healing Accessed 2023-04-02

20. Insecure Attachment and Other Help-Seeking Barriers ....https://www.ncbi.nlm.nih.gov/pmc/articles/PMC7313466/ Accessed 2023-04-02

21. The Relationships Between Self-Compassion, Attachment ....https://www.ncbi.nlm.nih.gov/pmc/articles/PMC5968043/ Accessed 2023-04-02

22. Self-Compassion Mediates the Link Between Attachment ....https://digitalcommons.unl.edu/cgi/viewcontent.cgi?article=2115&context=psychfacpub Accessed 2023-04-02

23. Identifying And Overcoming Unhealthy Attachment Issues.https://www.betterhelp.com/advice/relations/unhealthy-attachment-styles-types-definitions-and-therapy/ Accessed 2023-04-02

24. Adult Attachment Styles in the Workplace.https://digitalcommons.unl.e

du/cgi/viewcontent.cgi?article=1084&context=managementfacpub Accessed 2023-04-02

25. Attachment Styles: Definition, Types, and Theory. https://www.berkeleywellbeing.com/attachment-styles.html Accessed 2023-04-02

About the Author

Meet Shane "The Negotiator" Harris, an accomplished Tax and Accounting strategist, Business Coach, and a beacon of support for overwhelmed coaches, consultants, and speakers who strive for true financial freedom. With a remarkable talent for number crunching and an unwavering commitment to inspiring and motivating business owners, Shane offers personalized coaching and mentoring to help you succeed.

Hailing from New York and now based in Georgia, Shane's journey is rooted in service. She proudly served in the US armed forces and brings a background as a former nurse to her work. Before establishing her own company, Profit First Taxes, Shane gained extensive experience as a freelance tax preparer. Through her interactions with numerous clients, she discovered a common need for coaching among business owners. This realization led her to create Self B4 Abundance, a platform dedicated to empowering coaches, fostering clarity, and eliminating overwhelm. Shane's mission is clear: to guide you from being an employee to becoming the true CEO of your business.

Profit First Taxes provides virtual tax and accounting services to clients across the United States. The company's team consists of highly qualified professionals who prioritize integrity and professionalism in all their operations. They recognize the significance of meticulous documentation and legal tax planning in maximizing profitability. By leveraging their expertise, Profit First Taxes empowers clients to achieve financial freedom.

But Shane's role doesn't stop at taxes and accounting. With Self B4 Abundance, she provides online and in-person business coaching services, assembling a team of experts ready to support you in every step of your entrepreneurial journey. Her genuine desire to assist others is the foundation of her business philosophy. By paying close attention to your unique needs, Shane enhances your understanding and compliance with laws and regulations, ultimately leading to sustained profitability.

As your dedicated coach, Shane is committed to transforming your mindset and helping you achieve the financial freedom you aspire to. She believes your business's security and emotional well-being go hand in hand. With Shane, you can trust that your business finances are in capable hands and that she will guide you toward a future of success and fulfillment.

Take the first step toward lasting prosperity. Join Shane Harris on your path to financial freedom today.

A Gift for YOU!

www.ingramcontent.com/pod-product-compliance
Lightning Source LLC
Chambersburg PA
CBHW070517090426
42735CB00012B/2811